Nowhere Fast

William Kulik

saturnalia books

Distributed by University Press of New England
Hanover and London

Saturnalia Books
105 Woodside Rd.
Ardmore, PA 19003
info@saturnaliabooks.com

ISBN: 978-0-9833686-5-6
Library of Congress Control Number: 2012945503

Book Design by Saturnalia Books
Printing by The Prolific Group, Canada

Cover Art: "Turning Away" by Benjamin Schamberg

Author Photo: Donna Cossman

Distributed by:
University Press of New England
1 Court Street
Lebanon, NH 03766
800-421-1561

These poems have appeared in the following periodicals:

The American Poetry Review, a twenty-poem supplement to the May/June 2010 issue and the following in prior issues: "Colloquy," "Fictions," "Flexible," "Hi," "Dinner," "News from Nowhere," "No Recourse," "Old House Blues," "Whenever I Want You;" *Black Warrior Review*: "Hypereducated," "Résumé," "The Triumph of Narcissus and Aphrodite;" *Cimarron*: "Hanky-Panky," "Nowhere Fast;" *Miller's Pond*: "In the Bank;" The Prose Poem: "Obit:" *Volt*: "Final Solution."

"The Triumph of Narcissus and Aphrodite" also appeared in *Best American Poetry 1999*.

Table of Contents

"...to learn that a man has said or done a foolish thing is nothing, a man must learn that he is nothing but a fool, a much more ample and important instruction."

—Montaigne

ASK TIRESIAS

"Woman in the red hat, second row...you want to know about *what?*...those Trojan war heroes...what they were *really* like?...Glad you asked. I've always wanted to pull the plug on some of those guys. Take Achilles: a brat and a whiner right down the line, like a pro athlete who sulks if he can't get everything he wants. Hero my ass! Hiding out disguised as a woman. HE was the first draft-dodger, he and his buddy Odysseus, who tried to prove he was an idiot to keep from going to war. What about who?...Penelope? Was she *really* faithful? *That* broad? Don't get me started. And the tapestry act: what a scam! All those handsome rich guys hanging around and she didn't sleep with even *one* in twenty years? Lady, you believe that, you got to have been born yesterday...Next question; man in the front row...You want to *what?* Hear it from the horse's mouth how I got to be blind? OK, it was like this. Word. No myth bullshit: I'm out for a stroll after a three-retsina lunch when I come upon a pair of sacred snakes fucking—Delphic reptiles, if memory serves—and got me a nice set of titties for the next seven years...yeah, you heard right. So pissed I'd seen them they changed me into a woman (Ovid nailed this one, though take it from me most of the time he was full of shit).) And I'll tell *you,* just as I did the boss's old lady, Big Hera herself—may she strike me deaf if I'm lying as she did blind when I told her what she didn't want to hear. That Zeus was right: women do get more pleasure out of sex than men do. Much more!— or haven't you noticed? Look: a man comes once, maybe twice an hour, maybe a couple different times a day, maybe even three-four times, but that's maximum. Correct? Let me tell you, when I was a woman I'd come fifteen, maybe twenty times *a half hour,* several times a day, more if the guy was really hot. And, let me add, without the fears I had when I was a man: could I get it up, would it be hard enough, etc...Next question. You sir: can I *what?* Tell you if you're going to land that new job? Sorry, no prophecies today. Come back Tuesday...You, madam...do I have any advice about selling your home? Do I *ever!* Glad you asked"

WHAT HAPPENED IN PRE-HISTORY

After an hour of slow sweet sex with his personal trainer, old Triton felt a wetness down below, saw his horn sliced and the wine-dark water turning red but when he howled, "You have neutered me!" the young thing whispered in honeyed speech "Why, darlin', you must be mistaken: you KNOW nobody can unman a man but the man himself"

What could be better? The young guy had asked himself getting all that nooky and rare roast beef right up til the moment when the queen turned the girls loose. *Yes baby, it WAS a very good year,* she had said to him, clear-eyed and pitiless, *It's just how we do things here—plus you KNEW what the deal was when you signed on.* Even so, she feels a touch of regret watching them chase the old king through the forest howling for his balls. Then with a shrug and a tiny smile she puts a dab of perfume between her thighs and orders a bull slaughtered for the new kid in town

TALES FROM THE PENNSYLVANIA WOODS

CULTURE

Did you say "jeans?" Reminds me of the time I'm in Sullivan County with Tom having a cold one at the Laporte Hotel, six trout on ice back at camp when in comes this chick with THE tightest jeans on I've ever seen and who hasn't seen plenty of them? She's with a girlfriend, both dark-haired, nice makeup, all perky and joking with Jake the bartender. Right away all the guys come up out of their beers, suck their guts in, nobody watching what has been a really good ballgame. "What can I gitcha, Marie?" Jake asks and she says "the usual" and while he's pouring her a lime vodka with a squirt of grenadine, she's at the jukebox, hips rockin', fingers poppin' looking for "Her song" which turns out to be Mel McDaniel's 1984 chart-topper, "Baby's got 'er blue jeans on." Tom looks at me and rolls his eyes. She slides a quarter into the pool table, her girlfriend racks and after a break as powerful as any man's that sinks three balls, Marie proceeds to spend a lot of sweet time sizing up her shots, pouting and frowning at each and every one, hand on thrust-out hip, to finally bend way down over her cue, back perfectly flat and—why else all this prelude?—her round butt showcased in those super-tight jeans, the eyes of every guy in that boondock bar wired to her ass same as a bunch of art-lovers at the Metropolitan Museum in uptown Manhattan ooh-ing and ahh-ing over Aristotle Contemplating the Bust of Homer

DIFFERENT STROKES FOR COUNTRY FOLKS

The fat fire chief from Gaines, drunk on Slippery Nipples, tells the busty barmaid she's a shoo-in for a job if her tits touch the wall before her nose while she surreptitiously touches herself watching the square-jawed guy in a black cowboy hat who's got his hand on the thigh of a guy in full camo, when the tour bus dumps a hundred eager leafers who crowd the tiny bar, gawking. "Nothing in here," their disappointed leader says while the cowboy and the hunter hold hands and smile for a hundred cellphone cameras. "Say cheddar!" "Gorgonzola!" "Bleu!" "I'm from Wellsboro, you dumb fuck," says the barmaid. "I still bet your tits would touch first," says the chief, surreptitiously fondling himself

A FOOL FOR THE CITY

SAVE THE LAST DANCE FOR ME

It's party-time at Haddon Hall, *the* address in this town and I'm down and out, dancing for pay with a robust woman my height who's whispering dirty things in my ear. "Sorry," I say, "But I never sleep with anyone who outweighs me." A blonde about five-five with high-riding breasts and eyes clear as glass waves a ticket in my face. "Are you wearing a bra?" I ask. When she doesn't blink, I realize she's blind, and I want to tell her I've always been a fool with women and does she think it's possible to change. "No," she says, looking beyond me. "I'm not wearing a bra." We dance, her right hand, gentle and firm, in the small of my back

I WAS WONDERING

if maybe I should hit on one of the women grouped outside the Academy of Music waiting for the Fred Astaire retrospective but not sure whether razored poodle-cuts and chunky heels meant they were gay—still I needed to please them—so when they went for coffee I sat in the car afraid I'd get a ticket only to be jolted by a crash and then a flash of a '49 Caddy tailfin that in a blink swam in and out of sight and a plain but pleasant brunette rose from the spot where the fin had been, smiling nervously and whispering—very flirty, I think, for a legal guardian—"I guess you've got me."   And I come back with "That'll work. But I'm registered for pleasure use only." "I'll see you, maybe even raise," she says, writing herself a ticket for reckless endearment and flashing a glimpse of chunky heel

THE TRIUMPH OF NARCISSUS AND APHRODITE

Am I cool or an asshole? Check this: I'm at this artsy-fartsy cocktail party wearing a mauve turtleneck, white blazer, granny glasses and a tooled-silver peace symbol on a leather thong around my neck. Perfect for this crowd, right? I figure I'll test it out. So I lay some heavy eyes on this knockout blonde, about five-eight with legs up to here, and when she giggles and whispers in her girlfriend's ear, I read green and move on her, tearing a can from my six-pack. "So," I begin, popping the top. "What do you think of the new Pei student center?" The beer foams up over the edge of the can; I suck it swiftly, but not before some dribbles onto my jacket. She titters, brushing a Veronica Lake curl from her face. "O, I thought it was totally awesome"—a bimbo for sure, I think, with pretensions—"Form following function but with a dramatic sweep one ordinarily finds in the work of architects intending merely to outrage the sensibilities. And," she adds, "without the stark serenity of Aalto's last works, y'know? Like the Nordic ski facility he did for the Sibelius house." She tugs at her mini, I pull a lapel aside to show her my gut, flat and rock-hard from five workouts a week. She's got a foot-wide smile, best caps I've ever seen, skin flawless even in the glare of the floodlights. It's clear she's a cute little smartass who loves repartee, so I give her some: "Bet you don't remember Ted Williams' last game!" I go to straighten up, gain an inch, look even more imposing but my back has gotten stiff. It's these new shoes, I think. And the hostess must've dimmed the lights. That's cool: more romantic. Still, she doesn't look as clear-skinned now and her smile's lost maybe a little luster. "O I *don't?*" she comes back, a slight tremor and something savage in her voice. "He went four-for-four with a three-hundred-fifty foot homer his last at-bat ever!" She wipes a fleck of spit from her mouth. "And I saw every Ginger Rogers-Fred Astaire movie ever made. Stood in line the night they opened. Got the ticket stubs from each one." Her neck's thrust out at me and I could swear she's got a wattle. She's trembling with rage, but you know how cool

I am? Even with the sudden ache in my hands and the stiffness in my neck I manage to taunt her with something I think will stop her cold: "I useta party with Dante!" Is it getting darker? And somebody turned off the heat. Her girlfriend's gone and all the other guests too. There's just a guy sweeping up who stops and leers at us. It pisses me off some, but I lean forward to hear her cause there's this buzzing in my ears like a hive of bees, and I realize she's been yelling at me all the while. "Phaeton!" she screams. "When he drove Apollo's chariot across the sky and fell to earth in flames. I was THERE!" Her teeth are yellow and crooked, she's leaning on a stick, her clothes in rags. Now she's just an ectoplasmic outline, a grey halo in the cold dark. (Do I need a new prescription?) The walls are covered with moss. Water drips down onto the rock floor. I'm bent almost double, I can't see her at all, and all I hear is someone laughing. I stare at my shivering hand. There's my pinky ring. I'm still cool

LUCID DREAMS

I'm drifting somewhere in the Straits of Heartache when this sharp-featured guy with a Van Dyke beard appears saying, "Since there never was hope, which is beside their point—just part—and no kissing—they never mean it anyway." I drop anchor, bubbling with curiosity. "But Doctor Faustus," I plead, "Isn't it hard to give up the best love you ever had?" Now we're in a dark tavern in Bavaria where he takes a long pull on a double-bock and snorts, cartoon smoke coming from either nostril. "Overvalued," says he. "Cheap sentimentalizing—and shallow. If you'd heard as much shit from women as I have in the last six hundred years, you'd know better. All a means to an end. First lesson they learn in Chick School." He swings a leg over the seat to kick-start his '37 Indian: "We belong to different species." He guns her, gives me a low five and roars off. Goethe, sitting at the next table, smiles and winks. I wake up furious, a paddle next to me

Later that night I'm finally getting laid in a dream when these three guys straight out of a Max Jacob poem show up—identical hats, suits and faces—same ones who broke into the cell of Dumas *père* to steal the panties he sniffed to comfort him while he was doing time. I ask you what kind of jerk was I to let them into my pleasure-dome? Now I'm forced to watch as they cart my dream-lover off to the guillotine while as against my will I swim towards consciousness, unable to stop them

FROM THE ANNALS OF CHICK SCHOOL

A WORD FROM OUR BIRDS

She sets the plate down and watches him eat the quail whole. "Bon appetite," she whispers, untying her apron strings. "I'm through, finished, done, get it?" He sighs deeply. Both watch as wing feathers float into the darkness below the snow-white cloth

BLONDIE

Don't slice the cheese towards yourself is what he's saying at the very instant she gashes her belly and goes to the hospital where a handsome young intern who's sleeping with the head of surgery's wife and will die from colon cancer forty years later stitches her up but not without a remark about her navel-ring and a leer that prompts a grateful smile as she imagines driving the knife through her husband's breastbone

GLASS CEILING

("Come back to the office," he whispers, "We'll do it on the floor.") And she comes, in the full flowering of her belle-hood, proud to think that some day this bonehead will be the power behind her

Soon she's his private dancer, letting her long black hair fall below a five-ringed ear. Does she believe in revelation? Not when secrecy sans guilt is at the heart of her job description (And that, gentlemen, is Chick School Rule One and Only)

MORE WORDS ABOUT OUR BIRDS

CONCERTED

I'm at a retro heavy-metal concert waiting in line to use the port-a-potty when a blonde in Dazzy Dukes and a halter top, tattoo alligator curled around her bicep, cuts in front of me. The guy behind flings his arms up yelling "Yo, what's up with these broads? You gonna let her get away with that?" "What the hell you expect *me* to do?" I plead. "*We* expect you to leave us the fuck alone" comes the answer—in unison because now there are two of her, same top, shorts and alligator. Are there more on the way? I wonder as I watch them kiss, now fully aware of just how bad I've got to go

THERE'S THIS NOVEL NOVEL

in which Cool Ewell, a deeply endangered hero, swings from branch to branch crammed with chattering birds. "If I'm in a book," he thinks (though he knows what happened to "if") "I'm probably safe for now"

From his perch high in a gum tree, he watches a hen pheasant cross a field, as sure of herself as that woman who lifted her skirt for him one humid night

If he shot and missed, he knows she'd fly off, back in five minutes with no memory at all (The bird, too)

SITCOM

We're at our camp in the Pennsylvania mountains where cousin Don, electrician extraordinaire, is tapping into the local cable company's line so we can watch a special from Paris on Bolivian gold-mining narrated by a disgraced former High-White House official. What we get instead is us: Don wiring, me scratching my head. "What the hell is this?" he asks, pissed, switching channels. Now we have four women on a beach under a giant umbrella, laughing their asses off. Still not what we're looking for but "at least it's not us," I'm saying, though no sooner do I say it then who appears on the screen but me in a pair of bright orange trunks the women have turned their laughter on. "I was a fan of Holland in the '06 World Cup," I tell them, knowing it's lame, hoping this is just another bad dream I'll soon wake up from. "Dreams mean nothing to me," says a cute, dark-haired one wearing a teeny green bikini. "Caesarean?" I ask, seeing her scar. "Nope," she says, "I'm from Cleveland." Ignoring their titters, I press wildly onward, hoping green bikini doesn't notice I've cribbed Giacometti's line. "But if you read them right, dreams are true guides to psychic states, illuminating conscious life and at the same time, in the same symbolic shape they've assumed, giving clues to one's buried history, back to one's first minutes on earth, even—as Roheim insisted—to intrauterine life." I finish, staring at her scar. "Dreams are impenetrable," she says flatly. Plain old guffaws and thigh-slapping, which prompt me from the depths of my Tartar heritage to wish them good-day by burying them up to their necks in sand. "For daws to peck at," I think. "That's Shakespeare," the dark one replies, darkly. "He's impenetrable, too." Through peals of laughter—damned female thunder—I hear Don shout "Move, cuz, you're blockin' the screen"

FLEXIBLE

It's a beautiful day: sunny, crisp, cloudless. I'm walking down the boulevard in the middle of my life, just a tiny fist of apprehension in the center of my chest as I catch a glimpse of myself in a store window, reminding me I'm out looking for a camera to tape myself dancing because someone said I'm too stiff in the middle though I figure I'm OK for a white guy. So I find a shop: the owner is doing his best to fix me up but I don't see anything I like 'til his sister appears in a short red dress, displaying an expanse of gorgeous thigh. "*Consumers*' gives it a ninety-two," she says, thrusting a hip at me. "You're at least a ninety-two," I say with a dry mouth, "Maybe a hundred, but you must have a flaw somewhere." Her lips are very red and wet. "If you start licking," she says, "Maybe you'll find it." "Sorry," I say shortly, "but I've got a previous engagement"

And I do. Outside, under that brilliant sky, I'm on the ground with the store detective's thirty-eight against my ear. "Shoot!" somebody hollers. He cocks and squeezes six times. Watching me shake uncontrollably, he laughs. "You deserve this," she says, standing right above me, legs apart. My eyes trace the curve of her thigh 'til it disappears in the darkness. A voice whispers, "maybe if you were taller you'd get more." I think: that's it. First thing tomorrow, cowboy boots

KULIK'S TEN-THOUSANDTH DREAM

A woman sits on a green sofa with rolled arms, tiny blue porkpie hat perched on her huge head. As the I watches, she slowly spreads her legs 'til they're a hundred and eighty degrees from her torso, thick black bush aimed directly at him. His eyes fixed on the kinky hair, the poor guy's gorgonized, traumatized, paralyzed with fear she'll disjoint like a holiday bird and it'll be his fault! Then he notices— and this saves him for now—that her muscles are well-defined and glistening, as if she'd been oiled for a photograph like the ones he remembers from old issues of *Strength and Health*, ads for wheat germ or bone meal. Yes: just a pin-up in a gym, Big Mama staring down at a row of young men, supine, each one in a sweat to get two hundred pounds off his chest

MS. RULE

OF A FEATHER

Those Lewis women do something, they do it right. Like the party they throw when the youngest gets married; Meissen china, solid silver flatware and a ten-tiered cake baked by the Mayor's pastry chef. Such extravagance, but coupled with typical thrift: baked meats from the funeral of the dowager mother who has a fatal heart attack upon meeting the groom. Wearing the same stiffened look as the dead woman, the daughters quietly serve, studying each guest. But they shriek with wild laughter when the cotton cover is removed from what should've been the giant cake which they've replaced with a '72 Dodge Meadowbrook convertible, same vintage as the groom and, as he is now, shackled and yellow as the icing on the missing sweet. "Sharp car for a sharp guy," the oldest daughter says with a sneer, though the men don't notice as they are humming in unison a chorus of imagined muffler sounds. Her sisters, busy cleaning up, trade secret smiles, the bride's hand already on my thigh

THE BEST FACE

The doctor with the ritual scar tells me I'm going to die unless I keep my promise to the widow Janice to bring her husband Joe back from the dead so she can forgive him and reward me with a night in bed she says I'll never forget. Though I know this guy's a conjuror—and she's a tease—I'm certain I can pull it off. Besides, my skin's beginning to look like a butchered chicken's, so I don't have any choice. Just as I've got no choice but to drive my mother to an antique shop so—she says—she can buy something in memory of her late sister. We're barely there when I feel death's grip and I need to tell her what I've got to do. Instead, she drags me over to an oval mirror trimmed with horns and a tail. "Surprise!" she says, "It's for *you*!" Staring into the glass, I watch the pocked skin tighten on my skull. Shocked, I try to will a different face: rosy, less bony, but wind up looking as dead as the guy I'm supposed to save. And I can see clearly now I've got no choice but to confess, make a clean breast of it—plucked bird that I am. I should've known I never was going to get laid

THE ARISTOCRATS

It's always the high point of the show. My blonde lover, big and demanding, straddles me, dictating—as usual—position and activity: my face buried in her, lips on the huge floppy labia, tongue penetrating vagina, teeth nibbling clit. She's salty, which I'm used to, but never as wet as she claims so that, when she's had enough and moves down my belly licking and biting—not tenderly, I'd like to add—and pulls me into her, I shudder as she works the scratchy walls around the shaft of my cock. In the shadow of her bulk I do what I'm paid to until—this is the moment I dread—she takes it into her mouth and becomes a wiry, dark-haired man I must constantly struggle to will back into her shape. By the time it's over, I'm so exhausted I can only lie there, the ringmaster's shiny black boot on my chest, watching her take bow after bow, while the audience applauds fiercely. For as long as I can remember we've played to packed houses

PORN FABLE

Once, in the men's room at 30th Street Station, in the urinal next to mine, I saw a huge, stiff, throbbing penis. In a jealous rage I scrubbed it under hot water but could not bring it down to anywhere near my size. With bowed head I wept bitterly, my sobs echoing on the cold tile walls. And when I looked again—a miracle!—it was limp and very small, and in a voice as sweet and tender as a kernel of corn, it whispered: "My dear, do not envy what you cannot have. Live in the present and be content"

And so saying, it became a smooth, shiny pebble, grayish-brown and flecked with amber, glowing in the palm of my hand

HOT GIRLS

LYNN FELLOWS

My geeky friend's geeky friend, me, was awed by his big sister, two years older, two inches taller—and no acne!—who played field hockey, wore a thick maroon letter-sweater and had the first Woman's Ass I'd seen on a girl. I still recall the electric feel of standing behind her in their little dining room, staring at that round rear end in those tight dungarees, repeating her name in my mind, drawing it out: LLLLLLLYYYYYNNNNN, the silent sound traveling with my eye the line that curved down and outward from her hips, then tucked under, tightening where flesh tensed fabric, arcing up the seam that divided her cheeks, then down again: tighten, tuck and curve—after fifty years the circuit still piercing an incurable adolescent heart

FORTUNE TELLER

A leaf falls from the oak above onto your sidewalk table. You study its veins: lifeline, fateline, luckline wondering if maybe the pretty blonde a table away, eyes locked onto yours as she crosses her legs, putting lipstick on, would like to have her fortune told when suddenly the snake you can't deny slips from your mind, glides across the space between you, winds around her legs and vanishes in the dark bush she has, with a tiny smile, given you a glimpse of

THE EYE BEHIND

Our secretary: what a girl! You never know *what* she'll do next. Like coming to work in a blouse two sizes too small, two top buttons undone. Even better, with no skirt on; just a pair of ice-blue panties she keeps tugging at, snapping the elastic where it circles her upper thigh, right beneath her cute round ass with its tight little tuck (especially in those four-inch stilettos we love to see her wear). Imagine what it's like to watch as she fingers the lacy waistband, drawing it slowly down to reveal her pubic hair, thick and dark (or is it thin and light?). As she goes about her tasks—filing, taking dictation, reading email (who, we wonder, *is* sending her all those messages?), her silky brown hair (or is it blonde?) falls lightly on her shoulders. But it's equally possible it could be tied in a bun or braided or fastened by a glittering black clip, an exotic Polynesian comb or an elegant silver chain that barely tinkles as she parades back and forth all day long, the sensuous apprehension of baby eyes upon her

BAD BOYS

IRRATIONAL GEOGRAPHIC: THE WANDERER

I can flex butt-cheeks all day, waggle my huge impenitent member, but what's the point if no one thinks I'm hot? Solid and steadfast as the rhododendron I love to browse, I must go willingly when I'm tagged, wired and transported by Women Organized Against the Elk, who say I'm obdurate, intractable and worst of all, will not fawn. While they're totally correct, do they also know I'm kin to spirits in alder and oak, high priest of resins stiffening into wood? For sure, I'll embarrass the rest of the herd, emitting signals none of us comprehend. But as long as I still enjoy barging into picture windows and upending small cars, I'll get by

HANKY-PANKY

"For toads to knot and engender in," said the man, speaking of cisterns; the Big O, not as black as his lady's handkerchief was white. A class act in Venice but only, after all, a hired gun, another general, nothing to the Doge, wedding city to sea once the Turks were dispersed. And finally, just one more dead African, borne off beside his dear bride, Desdemona, and her Emilia, loyal but a little dense. "Ladies should look to their linen," the 18th century said, its dear classical unities ignored

I only knotted once with a toad, at least as I recall. And never with royalty; but my list of engendering's pretty steep: five kids, three abortions, too. And, though I never led an army, I was sucked off in a cistern by a general's brat. So all in all, I still think I'm a class act as, in my velvet-collar herringbone—Lord Chesterfield, the Neo-Classic age himself—I blow my nose in a handkerchief and never look to see what's there

"ARCH OF TRIUMPH" (1948)

I don't know if you know this flick but in it Ingrid Bergman dies to the usual violin background and sentimental soft-focus of a '40s movie while Charles Boyer whispers sweet lies to ease her passage, lines like "I couldn't have gone on breathing another hour if I hadn't met you" and "Though you slept around, I know that didn't mean you wouldn't come back to me at dawn, with another's kisses clinging to your lips." And why? I still don't know what you saw in me, a mere surgeon with a *de* before my seven-hundred-year-old family name: as if I really *was* somebody, though it's clear that without your love I had no title to even my wretched corner of earth, lost as I'd been in the shadows of the past, groping for my dreams of yesteryear, unaware we'd meet one rainy night in that smoky bar on the eve of war with Germany. And now I say—or rather I, the ghost of Charles Boyer, summoned by Kulik and speaking though the medium of this poem say—when you wandered from me, only to return after three years, dying, just as my character began to feel you might be losing interest in him, now (I say again) kneeling at your bedside, smoothing the covers, fluffing the pillow in the half-light of a tiny lamp, with those goddamned violins scraping away, my screen career shot delivering stupid lines not even a lovesick teenager could take seriously, laughing inside as you close your eyes for the thousandth fake movie-death and thinking of the question I wish I could've asked the dying you: "How many Nazis did you have to screw before you could afford that gorgeous Egyptian-cotton dust ruffle?"

EXPLICATION DE TEXTE

"Women are scary," pop tells me early in the book. Which helps explain why, with the details of exposition—birth, childhood, formative years—out of the way, the author makes me a lover of French culture, a student of *le grand geste* who searches for self-confidence in that *je n'sais quoi* of the *savoir-faire*, the nonchalant acceptance of *what is* that the heroines and heroes of Gallic film and fiction so aptly project. No longer a novel of growth and education, it's now a study of the unyielding ambivalence at the human core. Which is why he has me, a so-called adult, fall in love with a woman I meet one rainy afternoon in a bar called *L'atmosphere* near a bridge across the Canal St-Martin, Third Arrondissement, and hints I'll do whatever it takes to make me hers. I begin simply but with great care: almond croissant and *café brun*, then a Gauloise, which I practice dangling from my lower lip; and, in front of the mirror, wearing a dark-blue double-breasted chalk-stripe, imitate the insouciance of Yves Montand. Soon after, you're asked to believe I'm galled when, click-clacking down the rue de Rivoli in four-inch stilettos, she stares right through me, butt wig-wagging in her tight red mini. Then he writes what I consider a really boring chapter that pictures me devastated, seeking help from Freud, who tells me what I already know; that I am (quote unquote) a flop with chicks, ending my therapy with the question "What do *you* think women *really* want?" and smiling when I blurt out "Each other!" The key phrase that unlocks the real *me*. From then on the action picks up as through several well-paced scenes in glossy Parisian boutiques, I make genuine progress: the *de rigueur* little black dress, T-strap pumps, silver bracelets, even a diamond choker for the Big Date. One sunny afternoon towards what feels like the end of the book and ready as I'll ever be, I see her with girlfriends at a sidewalk table, rue du Cloche-Perce, that wonderful tangle of crossed legs, nylon glistening in the light, prompting a tiny *frisson* it takes the author two pages to analyze. Meanwhile I'm getting the sense of what a female feels in heels and a tight dress, taking little mincing steps like an Ungaro model, pausing at a table next to theirs where I sit half-turned to her, hoping I've been given a classic profile, and pretend to be interested in a conversation with a Piaf look-alike about perfume, orgasms and where in the Marais one finds the best champagne cocktail. Before I can sneak a peek to see if she's looking, he ends that section and takes the reader back to what he considers a trauma in my childhood: during the war, I'm alone with mom who smothers me with love, binding me to her while pop's installing torpedo-detectors in merchant ships, whoring with Danish captains and drinking hundred-year-old brandy with the barman at Antoine's. By the time he's through with his stupid digression, I've missed my chance. And the women all look like Charles Aznevour in *Shoot the Piano Player*: baggy coats and hangdog jowls, Gauloises hanging from their lower lips. Freud's there too, in morning coat and spats, notebook open, listening to them complain. I'd swear he winked at me, the dirty old man. A lot he knows

NO RECOURSE

It's my last day on earth and a guy in a white coat I hope to Christ is really a doctor and not some paranoid asshole escapee from a nuthouse is asking me intimate weird questions about my medical history, writing the answers down on a clipboard with a crude holographic likeness of a winking Mona Lisa who looks, I think, like Kirk Douglas in drag, taped to the back. Because my tenure here is tenuous, I don't respond to his steady stream of insults—though I am sorely, as they say, tempted to—as he mocks the scars, sags and creases of a body I've always hated. "Ugly black mark, right thigh," he demands, pointing with his pen. Grudging but obedient, I answer: "Pencil stab, kid brother, 1951." "Why?" "Teased him." "About what?" I feel a mixed rush of anger and shame. "Being a sissy." He scowls, and I wish I could shove the pen up his ass, but I need to give in. "Jagged scar, left eyebrow," he says, fingering the hair, and in spite of myself I get an odd tingle. "Highschool gang fight," I answer, remembering the sneer on the face of the kid who started it by calling me a queer. He pauses, staring deep into my eyes, then goes on about the folds of belly fat, the misshapen navel, the lopsided ears, the crooked chin, and I'm feeling less like a man than ever and more like his *minion*—the word comes to me out of a blue much like his eyes—so when he smirks at the patch of psoriasis I've always been ashamed of, it's more than I can bear. "Singed by the high-tension wires of life," I lisp, limp-wristed, and stare into those depthless, captivating eyes, which suddenly gleam with lust. Swiftly licking his lips, he yanks off a rubber mask: it's our twelfth-grade English teacher, Dr. Sonnenfeld, who we all thought was having an affair with the custodian, Mr. Delp, and here he is at heaven's gate with my fate in his hand, which is now behind my back and me without a single hymn to sing

FOUR FOR MAX

ONE: PLANET OF LOST HAIRMEN

Max Jacob and his soldier-boy, equally chrome-domed, aloft in a Nieuport twin-wing, wind streaming over the cowl in brilliant spears of light, his Isadora scarf free of the stick of their violent love a thousand feet in the sky. Back down, mugging for the press, the grinning guardsman makes a V behind the sunburned crown of the poet who raises a finger to silence the crowd of media clowns gathered for what their editors hope will be a great headline: MAX OUTS HIMSELF DECLARES UNDYING LOVE though it's equally possible he's about to wipe that spot of something hardening on his chin

TWO: MAX IN PENNSYLVANIA
for Susan Fleshman

Paradise, Blueball, Intercourse—what kind of jokers are these Amish? Is there maybe Phallus or Clit? He twitches the reins to remind the horse pulling his black buggy to step it up as he is meeting Liane and the Prince for lunch in Lancaster. Are there gay Amish, he wonders, smiling at two boys in black hats and suspenders, white sleeves rolled above the elbows, forearms bulging. Probably compliant, he thinks. Compliant but incurious

THREE: A POEM IN YOUR STYLE

He is desperately sick, beyond the help of anyone but the Asian crone in the next room lecturing on antibiotics. Does she have stronger medicine than his? Only diets, she says, and only for the faithful. Is he one of them? The huge oak door slides shut on gleaming rails. Then the lights go out. The smell of brown rice sizzling in tamari hits like the slap of his first doctor. Suddenly old and starving, he gropes in the dark, waiting for an answer

FOUR: HOUSE RULES

We're just back from the Zen Lesbian and I want the kids to meet Max Jacob, the famous French writer, who's reeling after six Kahlua-and- creams. So as not to wake the landlady, we take off our shoes, but Max drops one and suddenly she's there, arms folded across her chest, huge and implacable in her nightgown. He gives her a goofy grin, slowly sinks to his knees, then leans forward and vomits on her feet. She stares down at him, studying bits of half-digested pork, then glares at me and says. "I thought I told you *no poets*!" Max smiles and in his turn says "Tell hare I vant une blonde de haut taille...beeg like hare. Eat some now," he says, noticing the pork. "Save ze rest pour later"

DINNER

When I sit down to dinner, that wife of mine she comes and stands beside me and she says, Jack, you want to drink beer with your dinner? And I look at her and say, Well, what do *you* think? Do *you* think I should have some? And she says, Well, you always like beer with your dinner. So I say to her, Alright. You convince me. Bring me some beer. Then she says, You want Ortlieb's or Schmidt's? Schmidt's, I tell her and she brings a bottle, a quart bottle and a glass. She fills the glass and puts the bottle down beside me. I take a drink. It's good and I tell her I think it is. Now she says, will you have some whiskey? I look at her and I say, Yes I think I will have some whiskey. Will you get some for me? I will not, she says. It's right by your foot and you can get it yourself. I know this because I always keep it down there where I can reach it when I eat my dinner. She asks me then, What kind of glass you want, a water glass or a shot glass? Well, you woman, I say. You been married to me thirty years and you still don't know I can't drink a whole glass of whiskey with my dinner? So she brings a glass and fills it and I drink some, and then I drink some beer. The wife she asks me Is it good? And I tell her Yes. It is good. And I finish the whiskey *and* the beer. She fills both glasses again and asks me do I want my dinner. I tell her Certainly. And she brings it to me. It is veal. Veal scallopini with a big dish of French-fry potatoes. And a salad. A big toss salad, and rolls and butter. A plate of spaghetti, a dish of lima beans. First I eat the veal, then the spaghetti and then the French fries; then the lima beans the salad and rolls. And last I eat the lemon meringue pie. Then the wife she comes and stands beside me and she looks at me. I look at all the dishes. I look at her. And then I ask Is this all I get?

RÉSUMÉ

It's a typical Friday night for a couple of old marrieds. My love and I have just watched what a major network has been pleased to call an in-depth look at the '60s, we're waiting for the coq au vin to reach a perfect state of doneness, the fire is crackling merrily and, after three glasses of superb California Chardonnay, I'm feeling quite expansive. Which means, since classes have not been in session for three weeks, when my darling asks me the origin of the term "unisex," I can't resist waxing eloquent: "One of the great achievements of advertisers was to capitalize on the rhetoric of the human equality movement, co-opting what was novel if not outright revolutionary by playing fast and loose within the territory of sexual organization—dangerous ground indeed—where the absence of culturally-mandated, precisely-detailed rituals of passage to man-and-womanhood, made it possible for them to assert their power, implicit in the innuendo of text and body language, to sell us back our identities which that alienated, profit-at-all-costs economic and social matrix they had spoken for had been a primary instrument in destroying our sense of." I paused to drain my glass. Smiling at me in unfeigned adoration, face ruddy with firelight, my sweetheart fiddles with the radio, settling at last on a folk-music station. I pour us another glass of wine while we listen to Pete Seeger's inimitable rendition of "We Shall Overcome," from the Town Hall Concert, 1963. "How ironic," I hear myself say, unexpected sadness coloring my voice, "for it's increasingly clear we won't. At least we haven't to this point, and I see no indication that we will. In fact," (here I began to recall the heroes of my student years and those moving moments we shared on the ramparts) "a window may have closed permanently on our opportunity; perhaps even the ferment of the '60s was little more than an illusion created out of a need to convince ourselves there was actually hope for a democratic future, an exercise in wishful thinking driven no doubt by our parents' Depression dreams of solidarity and equality, themselves illusions engendered and sustained by their deeply-felt need to believe in socialist ideals." My love gazes up at me, wide-eyed and lascivious. "Did you say 'high heels?' It's just like him, the little scamp: sex over politics every time

THE POLITICS OF EXPERIENCE

When the Civil Anguish ended, I bought the Captain's jeep, a World War II number, full camo. "But sir, he isn't one of *us*!" his sergeant warned, as I drove off admiring the Captain's fake smile clinging to the rear-view mirror, out of which I could see my true love tearing after me in her daddy's '55 Nash with the fold-down seats we called The Sex Machine the summer James Brown made it a hit and I made her in it on the bluffs above the bad part of town where the Civil Unrest that led to the Civil Anguish had begun. The sergeant was right: I was not a man to trust, as I'd helped trigger the whole mess. It went like this: my true love and I are buying crustaceans for a soiree her mother was having for the canasta club right after the new laws which sparked the first acts of rebellion had been enacted. "Shrimp, lobster, crayfish," I say to the pinched little counterwoman. "Put them in alphabetical order," she orders, "Or I won't process your order." "Fuck thee and thine," I say, recalling my Quaker roots. "That's Quaker *oats*, man," says a hippy in a dirty red bandanna. "Oats are the next counter down," pinched-woman says, tugging at her shoulder holster. "Move along." "Wha'd you say, bitch?" he says. "I say that's hate speech, you clown," she snarls and quick as that she outs with her magnum and BAM! Down he goes. "One and done," she gloats

Which is how the Anguish began, ending only when the Oligarchs rescinded the odious Supermarket Edicts. Right now, though, running light after light, her right on my tail, all I could think of was *her* tail plopped on the seat of the Nash. Even though we'd been estranged since the start of hostilities owing to our political differences—she was for the underdog and I for her underwear—I still hoped we could reconcile, long enough at least to see if those Nash seats still worked. She pulled up beside me, rolled down the window and gave me the finger. "Say," I say, "What do you say we get a couple of Forties and get down?" "You can get down on your sister," she sneers. "Which reminds me," I say, "Your mother still owes me for the fish" and drove off, watching the Captain's smile become a frown

IN THE BANK

Like a lot of Americans, I was raised to believe that money is, as the rich say, "to die for." So you know I panic when a teller tells me I have nothing left in my account. When it turns out no one else does, rioting begins. Instantly, a SWAT team appears, led by a tall blonde in thigh-high boots. "I know you're head of this conspiracy to defraud," she says, though I hear "defrock" so when she whispers, "You're under house arrest," I wink and grin. "Your place or mine?" Her eyes widen. "Let's do it," she coos, "let's fall in love." Too late now: the troops have lined everyone up by gender, race and age, and are marching them into the vault's gleaming jaws. We watch the slow parade as June's golden sun becomes November's icy rain. She turns her worn face to me, forcing a smile. "For love or money," I think with a shiver. Outside, limos glide the boulevards. I notice she's putting on weight

RELIGION AND THE RISE OF CAPITALISM

When the anima came to town one summer night as a royal purple Rolls, we were beyond ecstatic—but the wind of belief soon blew cold and she hadn't packed her icons: not one mandala! So when they put her up on blocks and pulled her wheels off like some hillbilly Dodge, no one was really surprised, though lovers cried when they started parting her out. "Hey, you assholes!" someone screamed, "This ain't no junker hag; it's the *queen*, your immortal soul!" Silence. Then a greasy head popped up from under the hood. "For real?" it asked. "Then here's her regal bearing" and whipped one past our ears. We might've rushed him but we froze, so when the sun came up and we couldn't even cast a shadow, no one was really surprised, not even when we heard a Vegas wheeler-dealer had made her part of his vast display of what he called "outworn relics"

HOW DARTMOUTH GOT ITS NICKNAME

In which the roots of anti-Semitism are laid bare

"Old Jewbaiters," that's our private joke name for the acting club I joined when I was in college some years back, having come East with the blessings of my family, two generations in wholesale hardware, their expectations being that after studying the ins and outs of the usury business I'd return to become—I'll say this because you believe it anyway—the Shylock of the Twin Cities. In my chosen disguise, of course, which is why I, like others of my persuasion who were in the know, immediately joined that most secret of campus societies which, were I to tell you its real name— even now, in this venue—the Brothers would slash the tires of my Lincoln and send a thousand pepperoni pizzas in the shape of the Star of David to the Protestant Hospital for Stomach Cancer in my name—which they would swear is Israel Segal, distributing documents to the newspapers as proof. "Reality is mystery/ So how can we know History/Unless we make it up?" The key syllogism in the vows of fealty we took, smearing each other's foreheads—may God forgive me!—with the blood of a freshly-killed pig. Secret of secrets! But what wasn't based on secrecy, deception and fabrication in that remote northern college? Including its once-notorious reputation as a haven of anti-Semitism, which I swear on my mother's grave the Old Jewbaiters were responsible for creating and disseminating. That, and the nickname of its teams, "the Big Green," which you might think refers to the jerseys those vicious, huge, Gentile football players wore, or to that rich wilderness the campus is set in. But it doesn't stand for either, nor does it refer, as the most elaborate of our inventions would have you believe, to the supposed Irish roots of the founder who was really a Jew *posing as an Irishman* trying to pass himself off as a true-blue beef-eating Englishman. Add to this disguise a flawlessly-tuned British English which every so often would lapse into just the hint of a brogue and who wouldn't be convinced? Then, to complete the cast and ensure that the play would go on, connivance with a Rachel (also in disguise) who would marry our Semite poseur and give birth to the man—now a legitimized WASP but with the rumor of his Irish roots still trailing him—who would sign the Declaration of Independence. And members of every generation of Jews, down to this very day, have been in on the hoax, each adopting the mask of the last, eager for the promise hidden in the rapidly-become-naked forests of the New World: acceptance, respect, power and most of all money—the Big Green—not to mention the pleasure we get out of fooling you goyim, infiltrating the highest echelons of American society, corporation and country club—but always hidden! And, over perfect Martinis and sumptuous roasts, we even circulate the lies you've always been so eager to believe: the cloven hoof and the tail—do they exist?—and if so, are they buried in the deep folds of the monogrammed towel draped over the suntanned legs of the lady of the manor sitting poolside, her Jew beak fixed—who knows how many times—by the world's greatest surgeons

NEWS FROM NOWHERE

for Chris Thompson

The in-laws are here, back from China where her daddy cut a deal
with the Red entrepreneurs to "harvest organs"—you like that
one?—from executed "enemies of the state" and he's tickled pink.
I've got my feet up after a long day at whatever I do; my second
monster vodka's kicking in and the smell of liver and onions
beginning to fry are cushions against the wife yelling at her dad
because Harry Woo—jailed by the Chinese government for eighteen
years!—said today the organs are removed before the prisoners
have died. And suddenly he's here, right on my TV, saying it,
followed by the six o'clock anchorman, a ringer for Rimbaud in the
famous—is it 1870?—photo, down to the wifty cravat that keeps
bobbing up and down on his Adam's apple as he launches the typical
nightly barrage of mayhem, extortion, abuse, adultery, abortion,
rape and the myriad violations of the public trust. Yes, my poor
Arthur, horrible workers for sure. One more drink can't hurt, I think,
watching Capital's weird messengers power up: ghostly dancing
underwear, a can of pop shooting over the Rockies—world's
greatest ejaculation in silver and green as I'm asking myself how *did*
three thousand years of western culture come to this? But no worry,
I've got one fine buzz that makes me laugh when a faded sitcom star
appears, peddling a digital camera. "Like to diddle her," I think,
feeling very witty, but even though everything's soft-focused and
fuzzy, I know that outside, in the big-city twilight—as reported on
TV—a knife-edge of psychopathy lies pooled on the sidewalk,
threatening to seep beneath my triple-locked door. "Darkness
visible," I catch myself mumbling, in the same instant happy I still
remember Milton when the new Country Queen comes on, big lips

mouthing her latest hit, "Bite my latex." Whoopee! Measured amount of cleavage visible, perfectly programmed to incite the likes of me: overworked and underfucked. But when I hear "Feel free to feel exactly what we want you to," I can't tell if it's me or the TV. (I hope to hell *I'm* not an enemy of the state!) God, now she's shaking it in my face... and I feel fine, really fine—bottle at my lips, tears of gratitude streaming down my cheeks—like Winston at the end of *1984*! I hear the liver sizzling furiously now and I ask you: what's *not* to like about dinner in America?

SUSCEPTIBLE

I'd just finished watching a heart-warming episode of the new reality show *When Beasts Fuck Each Other Up* in which a cape Buffalo calf is culled from the fleeing herd by a pride of lions and dragged to the river where, as two of them are about to rip him up good, his haunch is grabbed by a croc which starts a tug of war that ends when the herd, seeing what is up, comes back and one huge bull rushes forward, spears a lion and flings him in the air like a toy animal while the croc lets go, freeing the calf who's off and running with the herd— completely unharmed. And with my heart warmed, feeling all soft and mushy, I doze through ads for laxatives beer and fried chicken when I'm jolted awake by the sound of gunfire as the camera moves slowly over a city destroyed by war—bombed-out buildings and smoldering vehicles—then suddenly zooms down to an alley where a pack of Serb Christian soldiers are busy raping a Bosnian Muslim woman while her kids watch horrified 'til other soldiers come and bayonet them while the mother screams "Kill me! Kill me! Dirty sons of bitches!" Which they do right after the last guy in line gets his turn and we cut to an interview with an old Serb who explains through his tears how after centuries of war somebody always owes or is owed a death because someone in his family fucked up or was fucked up by someone in another family maybe two, three, even ten generations past. Why, he asks again and again, why, 'til I realize I'm crunching hunk after hunk of crap fried chicken, bones of tiny screaming humans a rampage of blood in the mouth of yet one more innocent man

BACKSTORY

The cook was in the kitchen searching for a recipe for grilled octopus. Done with Batali, Beard and Bobby Flay, she was about to reference the elusive Julia Child when her nephew appeared. "I want my money to grow," he grumbled. "No dear," she gently chided, "You must say 'I want to grow my money.'" He frowned while she looked out the window as a young woman in a Duesenberg replica hit a button and the tent-peaks on several miniature castles she was towing on a flatbed rose up and tipped their green hats revealing golden busts of famed prophets, chief among them Mohammed, his face veiled, Jesus looking soulfully at a light from above and Gautama Buddha extending his hand which held a ball, symbolic of earth and the four billion of us who crowd its surface. The cook's brother Steve, recently empowered and in no need of salvation, had eyes only for the young woman and, once inside her blouse, embarked on a vigorous search-and-grab mission she allowed to go on long enough for him to shut the bedroom door behind him, the same one she kicked open minutes later revealing a sordid tableau: he on top mashing her pretty round breasts, she struggling against his weight, legs flailing, her face twisted into a grimace equal parts anger and disgust. At last, with a huge upward thrust she gets him off her and, turning sharply, aims a kick that gets him in the throat and down he goes gagging and immobilized while she flings her dress on and speeds off in the Doozie with the prophets still exposed. The nephew watches his father panting on the floor and shakes his head in anger and disgust. "Maybe now you'll stop referencing the Marquis de Sade and help me grow my money." "Good boy!" chirps Auntie-the-Cook watching chopped tentacles curl in melted butter over high heat as she ponders the strange magic of an age of transition when yet another noun becomes a verb while active and passive quietly change places

IRRATIONAL GEOGRAPHIC: WHO MADE THEE

Once I was saved—poor little lamb about to be Easter brunch—my slit neck sealed by an unseen hand. Since then I've wandered very far, over land and sea, convinced these undulations in my chest are the wings of the Holy Ghost. Wherever I go, crowds gather to stare at the wound that never heals and the foreleg picked clean. I'm always grateful they don't laugh at my altar-boy clothes: stiff white shirt, black tie that drags in the dust of the road where I limp along—happy to serve, with one desire left: to someday lick the hand that drew the blade across my throat

GREEN-CARD GUILT

I've told you before, haven't I, about my dear immigrant, here such a short while yet so accustomed to my ways? And just on the brink of pardoning me for my last crime when I struck again, spilling honey on her best blouse. She was lying there so still I thought she was dead, and when I leaned over to see if she was breathing, my honey-pot tipped and the evil deed was done. Dear sweet immigrant, so new to my ways but savvy all the same. This time her punishment is to make me wear a pair of filthy smelly sneaks, the tops looking as if they'd been eaten by the wolves who raised me. And these red socks! She might as well have sewn a letter on my chest. To hide my shame, I've learned to walk with the toes of the back foot curled behind the front so each is only seen in flashes—though she tells me I'm fooling myself, that my living guilt is always visible, blazing like a Times Square billboard. And I don't have to tell *you* how I made things even worse using vinegar to get the honey off. Now she smells like a Chinese restaurant! Ah, my dear sweet-and-sour immigrant: so new to my world and already she knows I don't want to be healed

PRETTY-BOY-FREUD

Today I woke up shaken after a dream that made me realize some questions *do* run too deep—especially for this simple man. And with implied answers I won't dare to examine. It goes like this: a thirty-ish blonde is sitting with her beautiful legs crossed, smiling hypnotically—standard stuff except for a sudden Bride-of-Frankenstein herky-jerkiness as she flings off her top and her skirt, spreads her legs wide, pauses for an instant then smacks her knees together and—hello!—I'm nine years old under our kitchen table enthralled as mom and her girlfriend cross and uncross their legs, releasing the smell of perfumed thighs and though I pretend to be playing innocently with my little iron dump truck what I really want is to savage my sister's Raggedy Ann with it, pressing wheels red-hot from friction with the rug up against her imagined divide, a crazed kid shouting "VROOM! VROOM! VROOM!" until I tear it open fall on the cotton crotch gobble the fuzz shocked awake into the indispensable thrust of wild desire with hands that imagine they can govern the path of the oncoming truck

FICTIONS

for my brother Ted

In that novel you bought at the chain, a young woman looks back on her life. She's 30, a teacher married to a Harley-riding oil exec, mother of two sons. They have an apartment uptown, take exciting trips, but she's bored, frozen, galvanized into life only during rough sex or when she pictures him dying on one of his drunken, lights-off rides across the Throggs Neck bridge. She thinks, as you do, her dad may have abused her: dreams and flashbacks tell her it's true. Meanwhile he, driven by his own demon, is made by the author to describe their life as "a simple story of seduction, rape and madness, the usual preoccupations." Now deep in the book, you wonder if they're being readied for some sinister ritual the one will create, the other acquiesce in. You wish they'd come to grips but it's hopeless: he won't give up his rage against a cold, demanding mother, she the hold on reality perfect order gives her. When their fate is revealed, you applaud silently, a witness to the truth of those struggles that imitate your secret life so well you identify and are consoled. But are you liberated? Not likely, any more than if you'd watched the war that prompts those sounds of agony amplified by two huge speakers under the ring on whose sweaty canvas Killa Quadzilla meets Dr. Death in a world of faked falls, stomps and roars, the theatrical shame of the one about to be drop-kicked into the screaming crowd, the other suddenly real to you in the cocky strut and powerful hairy arms, hand on the helpless throat, you and your brother huddled in a corner of the room hugging crying Mommy daddy please stop we love you we're sorry

OLD HOUSE BLUES

for Amy and Alex

Everyone's here. And because I love old things, I've rented a grand Victorian in a part of town devoted to preservation, where even a splendid place such as this one—broad corridors and stairwells, dark, narrow arteries leading from room to room, each with its own period architectural marvels—is common. After a welcoming dinner, we walk the halls: floor polish, cedar, sachet—wonderful old odors—toward the evening's entertainment. On our way, we stop to admire each room's unique details. In the study, tales of Dionysius and his cohort molded on plaster cornices, Pan and Syrinx in a bedroom, garlanded by wreaths and berries and, on the drawing-room ceiling, the feature attraction: an oval painting of Echo and Narcissus. In each room walnut floors, cherry baseboards, carved oak mantels, all glowing with the magic of lost arts, of artisans long-gone. I order the house lights turned up to make everything clear, but am told it isn't possible: soon the show will begin. That's odd, I think, shivering as we arrive at the end of the house—doesn't the power reach this far? I open the door to the final wing: panic seizes me. Floors sag, lath shows through the fallen plaster. This'll take some work, I think, my spirits high as I recall the fortresses I'd made out of other houses that were vulnerable to roving gangs. But the jumble of wires on the floor, guitars and amps everywhere, make it clear my son and his friends have taken over. I try to persuade him to return to his room in the main body 'til I can get things back to normal, but he's adamant. "You're too serious, pops," he says. "Besides, the play's the thing." Seeing the empty bottles, the piles of crumpled Mickey D. and Cheese Doodle wrappers, I feel the panic again. Suddenly the lights blink twice and go out. From a darkened corner, stage right, a woman giggles. "The metaphor's trite," she says.

The audience titters. Smiling into the darkness behind her, I pat the lease in my breast pocket. "Try again, Kafka," she shouts. This time the laughter is loud. A few hoots. Twisting the top off a bottle of beer and popping a bag of chips, I wonder if something's over. "You bet it is, Big Daddy!" she calls out for a third time. Taking my cue, I step forward, bow, then turn and walk toward the curtains. Applause is general, but there are no encores: just the old odors—floor polish, cedar, sachet—and a single rose

COLLOQUY

On the verandah, fat scotch in hand, trying not to make sense of
another day in Nadaville, I imagine I'm telling my dead friend, Jeff
Marks, who knew me best, how as a child I'd lie in bed subtracting
the world, piece by piece: father, mother, friends, animals,
neighborhood; then Philadelphia, America, the oceans, earth and
sky 'til there was nothing left but blackness—and me, dizzy,
spinning, unable, however hard I tried, to subtract the mind trying
to subtract itself. And how, the night before last, I had a creepy
dream where I was stretched out waiting, staring, when my usual
face turned dinosaur-shaped and bone-white, as if the flesh had
been boiled off, the mouth exploding in a scream, and next day in the
garden, squashing Japanese beetles with my fingers, I saw that same
face on a bug who, I swear, stared at me, daring me to kill him.
Which, as I'm telling Jeff, struck me as a premonition, so I'm not
really surprised when Death, in traditional costume, appears at my
elbow. "These are positive signs," he says, "but I need more proof of
your commitment." "Like what?" I ask, annoyed that he doubts me.
"I read Beckett, load up on despair, try to be stoical: think of myself
as a ripe grape whose time to fall is coming, the way Aurelius says
to. I'm deep into Nietzsche on fate, Sartre on non-being, Camus on
suicide, what more do you want?" "Literary guys," he sneers,
showing a set of yellow teeth. "I know you only use those half-ass
ideas to appease me. Think you can hold me off with that bullshit?
When it's your turn, it's your turn, and the hell with Wittgenstein.
And incidentally," he says with a stare as cold as the moon, "it's your
turn." He spits the words in my face, breath so incredibly foul I
wince, my whole life rewinding before me. But pretty quick cause
it's so ordinary: the kids go from grown-ups to babies, I have my
hair back, endure the trials of marriage, the shy college years,
adolescent shame, the terrors of separation, all the way back to the
dark bedroom of the six-year-old who could make the world

disappear, only his consciousness left: and would this be the subtraction of *it*? Feeling a full-body tremor as I did the time a mugger held a thirty-eight against my temple, I hear a frightened voice begging, "please can I have more time? Maybe finish another book, live to see a grandchild?" He snickers, and I get another peep at the yellow fangs. "Deal," he says, "Just remember this." And he pulls back his cowl. What he shows me I can't describe except to say it's at the same time mind and not-mind and the mirror of mind shattered and reflected from a thousand constantly-changing angles, and out of that whirlwind of light came the barking of a thousand hounds. I squeeze my head—hard—to keep my trained animal from leaping its leash, hear him whisper, "au revoir" as, with the sound of a balloon running out of air, he vanishes, leaving the smell of garbage rotting in the sun

TWO FOR POP

ONE: FILIAL PIETY

I'm on the same bike my father rode into the void, pedaling hard, shouting to an empty sky, "Pop, I'm getting nowhere: You gotta help me!" and he's there at the roadside, same big nose and fine grey hair as mine, looking hard at me with his crystal-blue eyes. "Stop whining, sonny-boy," he orders, "you ought to know there's no *anywhere* to get to. Remember what Marcus Aurelius said, camped on the Danube, A.D.56? 'Be not perturbed, for all things are according to the universal; and in a little while you will be nobody and nowhere.' Got it?" My old historian! He disappears and I'm alone again, belly full of fear, pure nada on my dark path to the sea. And sooner than I'd like, I'm there, on a beach littered with bikes. Following the crowd, I wade in, surprised to find the ocean floor is soft, the water nearly weightless. My father's way ahead, riding the swells in the family inner-tube inscribed with Hamlet's line: "We fat all creatures to fat ourselves, and fat ourselves for maggots." He looks back, grinning. My old recycler! No time to grieve for all the things I wish I'd done: soon the wind picks up and tiny waves revolve us like fish asleep or merely dead

TWO: WHENEVER I WANT YOU

The old man again! This time we're going bear-hunting. He drinks from a pint bottle and shows me his prize watch, limp like Dali's 'til I look again and see it's only lopsided, but with tiny feet. The scenery goes by as in an old movie set, where the car rocks and the driver over-steers to persuade you it's all really happening, that there aren't fifty people—technicians, supporting cast, the director and his staff—just outside the borders of the film. This should be a big scene cause this is my pop, dead for twenty years, swigging away and holding that talisman, I want to call it, which I now see has white porcelain edges bisected by a red line like the one on the painted metal tables everyone in the '40s had, with extensions on either side that screeched when you pulled them out, meaning in our house: "Company coming!" Usually my late mother's sister Jennie, her husband Tony, their daughter Joan: all of them gone, Joan dying before Jennie—how did she bear it?—but the camera's on my father and me, together again, as in the old days in love with the hunt, always so much to discuss—if only he'd talked!—so much like his strange little watch that's now got the stick arms and legs of a cartoon character, an expression of frozen delight—or horror—mouth wide open that if it could speak would say

HI,

(in memory of Wolfman Jack)

My name's James, enlightenment's my game. Comin' at y'all with Soul Break, the two-minute hot spot on the hottest spot in town: WSLF Millenium Radio2000 on your dial where we know the pose of those who think the word can cut itself and you out there usin' Twoness to reach Oneness thinkin' you ain't really real with a capital R 'til you be like old Frog-in-Suchness—don't know his ass from his eyeball but give you one helluvva Chugarumph!! And do that jump-in-pond sound all y'all dig on—cause you be thinkin' he got somethin' you *don't* have, which is where you wrong and why I'm here tryin' to get in your Original Face, tell you ain't nothin' here to realize, actualize, fecundize: you can't *get it* cause you already *got it*, and if you *could* get it, it wouldn't be *it*, got it? Just you lookin' for the Ultimate's a joke! Hell, any state *you* could find wouldn't be Ultimate if *you* could find it, ain't I right? And dig this: what you in your Twoness call the illusion created by your Twoness which illusion you are usin' to reach the Oneness you in your illusion think you *ought to* reach—all that mess is what the Man, Brah-man, is already doin'; and, like the man says: "Console thyself, thou woulds't not seek me if they hads't not already found me." Now that's *the truth*. Ain't no illusion—but it's all there is for now, brothers and sisters in the Land of Pure Delusion. Time for James to park it on his little satin pillow, fold hands and stare at the dot he painted on the wall. Cause I got my own confusion. Night, y'all"

CAR TALK

Hello it's me, me and that other me, the puppet who never shuts up. Right now we're riding along the Delmarva peninsula on our karmic wheels in a never-ending but absurd search for meaning that we know in our heart does not exist. Ocean to the left and row after row of cute weathered cottages and to the right the Chicken King's domain: miles of hens body to body in long low sheds. I'm just cruisin' with the top down playin' the radio and repeating my latest mantra, "with the torches of chaos and doubt the sage lights his way," hopeful in spite of myself—even though I know it's vain to think it—that *this time* maybe I'll break on through to that other side where a mountain is just a mountain, mention of which reminds me of Dostoevski's emblem of survival: imagine (he says)a man with an incurable disease in a niche on a sheer cliff, battered by winds, no hope of rescue, still hanging on—in that quaint and out-of-date phrase "for dear life." "Trippy!" says the puppet, in 1968-speech "But *for what?* "Maybe five minutes more of the same old stupid shit?" which stings me cause I feel it's true and would love to pause and meditate on it but I'm already caught by a strong signal from the poultry world across the road: a clear picture of those pathetic hens, brief lives spent in savage pecking and flapping of stunted wings who in spite of which rise from the filthy straw to turn their precious eggs and keep the chicks from being born deformed. "But sweet Jesus, *for what?*" the puppet repeats. "To be slaughtered packaged and sold to some vacationing jackass who'll grill them on the deck of his cutesy little rental cottage? It's totally meaningless!" "What the hell is that NOT true of?" I hear me shout back. And neither I nor big mouth has an answer. Right now all I know is there are chickens to the right, ocean to the left and in front of me the road, a black belt vanishing over the hill. And no particular place to go

NOWHERE FAST

All the usual amusements: Whip, Tilt-a-Whirl, Tunnel of Love, and all the usual rigged games: Wheel of Fortune, Ring Toss, the pyramid of weighted bottles and the lopsided softball you could never knock them down with. We played hard anyway, all in fast forward, so when it rained, we raced through thick mud, laughing like madmen, and when the sun came out, brilliant, painful, we were nauseous from the cheap hotdogs and funnel-cake we'd wolfed. Now, ready to go, but with no access to the highway, we imagine we hear traffic speeding towards home. Our bus has vanished, and the solemn, dog-faced guard with his badge and magazine won't let us cross the bridge whose giant span arcs into a terrifying mist. Is it hiding our lovely town? With no choice left, we stagger to the ancient inn, its half-timbered walls bent and sagging. In the great hall, weary mothers nurse infants, old men trade blank stares children race in endless circles screeching. Our orders are suddenly coming fast: but what was whose? And where had I put my wallet? No I.D.! No matter. If I hadn't already ceased to exist, I soon would. Lucky kids with their mandated tattoos and the brand-new edict banning coloring books. No need for freedom or imagination as the cellular drama picks up speed, we now twitching like actors in the early days of film, while under the pressure of the blurred horizon rushing towards us, all our surfaces crack and flatten like an unrestored canvas. And there's no reprieve: soon nothing left but dust and a bracelet or two of bone. Children's toys, mementos of the fair

OBIT

He prays for another chance but the ambulance comes anyway, no roses or fanfare. The driver wants to know if the paperwork is right and why he keeps repeating "catastrophe...somnambulist..." Probably a decent guy who kept his pencils sharp. And lucky, too: women always coming on to him. A damn shame, says the man who pauses with his dog to watch the flashing light slice the branches on the old oak in front of the neat white house. Next morning over tea he tells his significant other someone died. Or maybe he forgets to

IRRATIONAL GEOGRAPHIC: TABLETS

A Catastrodemonologist suitably dressed in black is watching a sequence of white and blue neon-like lines pulsating in rhythm with my heart appear and disappear on a screen. "Cellular migration," he says, "Seen it a thousand times." A shock of hair-raising recognition runs its course in my bloodstream. "Is this the dread vitamin definitioncy?" The Big Cat laughs, dipping his whiskers in milk, and sends me to his friend, the Pharmacocaterwauler ("Lil Cat") with instructions to bring him back a feather to sniff during fast days. Slowly I drag myself to his office in the trees. Dressed suitably in grey, tail angled sharply towards the sky, he picks a blueberry from a branch. "Need medicine immediately," I cry. "Gimme pills!" He shakes his sleek head. "Poor schmuck," he peeps, "You useta take 'em all the time. Whydja ever stop?" "Dunno," I say, "Maybe that bus ride through the desert with an ancient dude in a tunic who kept asking me if I knew some princess down in old Cairo and trying to stick me with a needle put a spell on me." "May be," he agrees. "Except for the lousy syntax. Look, there's an Egyptology confab happening across the hall. You ought to get your sorry ass over there and see what they can do. And bring me back some locusts, OK? Just not the whole plague." I go, though I'm afraid I'll get double-crossed like that Christ guy or maybe wind up in an Osiris and Harriet re-run. Once the door closes behind me I know it's too late: ominous grey birds are everywhere and a bunch of gents in gold wearing funny headdresses and surrounded by black cats are playing faro and the house is cleaning up. A tall somber man wrapped in bandages and looking like he'd crumble if you touched him waves a scepter and beckons me to follow. It's the weirdo from the bus! Down the dank stairs I go, grudgingly grateful, following my specter into this Valley of Kinks, noticing some of the gold guys from upstairs are already here, side by side in a subway car, reading. On the walls are the famed secret writings, pulsating with the grammar of transformation. O to have been born Egyptian with the spring of life so near! "That's only half the story," the old crumbler says, handing me a stone copy of the Book of the Dead. O well, here we go again, I think, carefully writing my name in the flyleaf

HYPEREDUCATED

The night I re-read Schopenhauer I saw all my old ideas in a new light. As we drove downtown in our rusted-out wreck of a car, I felt alive with hope. Everything suddenly made sense. Eyes blazing, I told her "Living in the present doesn't mean having to obliterate the past but incessantly re-interpreting it in terms of what the future brings." The light was turning yellow as we drifted through the intersection. "Better hit that pedal," she said. I did, but the car only bucked and lurched. A cloud of blue smoke appeared and the smell of burning oil. "You need a ring job," she said. Next day we got married

REUNION

Coming down from the mountaintop, my secret still intact, I get sideswiped by a lovely lady in a raccoon coat hair bobbed á là 1943 though it's her breasts that keep me from pressing charges. Holding hands at the overlook, she claims it's love at first sight. "Don't *you* see?" she insists but all I've got eyes for is a baby boy being lowered into the valley in a wicker basket, his parents' faces big as billboards and hard as nipples in winter. Begging her pardon, I free my hand and go down into the dark forest where branches claw and creatures howl. I ask a twisted little man with a sinister stick who suddenly appears beside me if he knows where the kid is but all he's got for me is a load of bad advice. At dawn, limp with grief, I'm expelled from the woods into a clearing where my lady waits with a preacher who pops the cork on a bottle of champagne and whispers with a wink "You'll get used to it" while I fondle my new foot-long beard and ponder the miracle of our cars, now side by side—and not a scratch on either. "So this is the real deal," I mutter, knowing it's now or never. But when I start to speak she puts a shushing finger on my lips and whispers "No secrets." We've lived happily ever after, she says. Which I wouldn't doubt

BIRDBRAIN SINGS

"You want to know if I find *myself* guilty of the crimes I've been charged with? Absolutely, your Honor. And you want to know *why* I systematically destroyed what it had taken a lifetime to build? Simple: I believe I was destined to and which is why I love these lines from Emily Dickinson: 'How complicate the discipline of Man/Compelling him to choose/His pre-appointed pain'; and this from Schopenhauer: 'I can do what I will but not will what I will' which means to me, sir, that seen *sub specie aeternitatis*—with the eye of God—freedom of choice is pure illusion. But even if—as I believe—I had no choice, I understand I must be punished as an 'I' who 'did' what he did. And if I seem—as I know I am—all too willing to accept blame, it's because I identify with the character type Freud outlined in his great 1926 essay 'The Economic Problem of the Masochism' who, failing to get the degree of punishment he needs from the super-ego, is compelled to create reality situations so humiliating they can't be escaped from, his crimes verified by the community, his punishment to be tortured by guilt '*aller arten*'— unending, like the torture the pasha in Mozart's *Die Entführing aus dem Serail* declares shall be the heroine's fate after which she sings her beautiful aria. And speaking of which, this is the end of my song except for one last admission: that all my life I've had the dual thrill of Baudelaire's voice in one ear whispering, 'I am the knife and the wound,' and Nietzsche's in the other intoning, 'He who refuses to ⸀ ⸀e himself will never be strong. He deserves to die.' Your honor, ⸀ case. Do with me as you will"

GIVE ME LIBERTY OR WHATEVER

The cursor's playing hide-and-seek as she hurries to write down the details of last night's dream—which her shrink says she must if she wants to be free (even at that he guarantees nothing). She knows not everyone thinks 45 is tough, but she does. Her wrinkles ("of denial," the shrink says) as undeniable as that hint of a moustache, dark warning that has arrived in synch with the drop in estrogen levels and the birth of that tummy–fat she packs into her jeans. No winning this one, she frets, throwing another scale into the trash. But she still does fifty pushups a day and hits the machine for an hour, urged on by the photo of herself at 25 that stares down at her (frowning, she imagines). And with the dawn of her own New Age she's re-styled her hair to minimize a huge forehead (even though she knows it accentuates the prognathous jaw she feels makes her look like an ape). She's most concerned about a lurking urge to quit the hunt, just bring home the bacon, eat it all all alone, at the same time she's vexed because she can't escape the fantasy of a silken ladder that leads to the den of what may be the last remaining prince still in his immaculate frogness. And she's pleased that men still hit on her however lost they all seem. Unlike herself, she thinks, borne along on this journey by the Life Coach she's preparing to replace the shrink with his disturbing questions. "Feels like the Inquisition," she has breathed into the placid face of her new boy who ends each session with a tape of Gloria Gaynor, the disco queen, singing "I will survive," holding her hand as he holds her gaze whispering "and you will too"

LOST TANGO

for CVW

It's easy enough. Just picture yourself on that second-floor Latin Quarter balcony elaborate wrought-iron railings filigreed tables and chairs lush ferns the smell of incense and patchouli and for genuine retro-ambience Marek Weber's "Jealousy" pursuing smooth muscular legs in black tights. Same balcony the leggy Ellen Barkin cursing him like hell-hath-no-fury flings Tom Waits' clothes off of in that 1986 movie "Down by Law" that we saw a dozen years after we'd found the stacks of Weber tangos on a shelf in a closet of our first apartment left by an angry divorcee with two spiteful teenage girls. Still, we danced night after night to the scratchy 78s, very much in love. One thing I can't know is did she fill trash bags with my stuff in blind rage throwing out the least reminder of our years together? "Best legs in Philly," I always told her and she'd smile

IRRATIONAL GEOGRAPHIC: A DOG'S LIFE

"All men are dogs," my mother barked and moved out to live with a pack of angry ex-wives the old man called "a gathering of Lesbos." Too harsh, I thought, but in those days what did I know of the world or my place in it? And now that it would be just me and my misanthropic pop—a backward beast if there ever was one—my chances of learning to fit in seemed all but nil. Especially in Philadelphia, famed for hydrants and parks but notorious—at least in the canine community—for its rigid class structure. And there I was, a mutt from Poland, nose to the ground and zero status with those European pure-breds with pink sequined collars and perfect hair. Of course that snobbery would've been less a problem if I hadn't so totally absorbed the old man's social insecurity. Hiding behind the face I wore to meet the faces that I met, I felt like poor dad, a weak-spirited creature whose favorite expressions "Give us this day our daily grovel" and "Hide the bones, stay home and fuck 'em" made me so terrified of the dog-eat-dog world I chose the gentler life of academe, sniffing the tortured path all the way through grad school, licking whatever I was told to. Meanwhile, poor pop's alienation was complete: he grew reclusive, going out only long enough to lift a joyless leg, fearing and at the same time expecting a swift kick from a human foot, a prime example of what my studies had taught me to understand as "a climate of ambivalence"—and masochistic to the core. Still I wonder how the old mutt or any dog worth his bone could surrender the pleasure— and the memories to treasure—of sniffing hems and stockings. Especially, in yours truly's case, those black silk ones that cling to the shapely legs of my latest love, a charmingly tenacious West Highland terrier. But I have to go slowly, as my need to succeed after so many failures ("All men are dogs," say my five ex-wives) may cloud my judgment, and the dark truth is that even the sweetest memories remind one that time present and time future are becoming time past in the very act of recollection. And finally, despite how far I've come—a PhD in Canine Studies and a prestigious job teaching the pets of the rich and famous—I'm no bulldog like T.S. Eliot, who braved as he put it "the awful daring of a moment's surrender," even less a Wittgenstein, that sleek Whippet prince of philosophers. Though his famous question, never far from my thoughts, reminds me how prone to fallibility we all are: "Is my understanding only blindness to my lack of understanding?" And thereby droops my tail

DIVESTMENT

I don't know about your teacher but mine's picked the Extended Life plan where you're guaranteed additional years as long as you agree to surrender any further claim to women, including even memories of being driven mad by girls' bodies, all us guys united by the lust that keeps that market up. "Overvalued," says my teacher, "Biggest of all the bubbles," his entire stock now in books and blackboards, his spare time spent pondering Peggy Lee's question: "is that all there is?" Yet in spite of the contract, he sometimes feels the old urge rise—teased to life by a student in the third row with her legs parted or one with her tramp-stamp showing. And in those guilt-riddled moments he sees himself on a re-make of "This is Your Life" hugged by ancient friends—stooped but smiling through perfect choppers—and with them someone's great-granddaughter, a 20-year-old in short skirt and tight top with a neckline that plunges so deeply only her nipples are hidden and he dreads the moment when Ralph Edwards shouts "Everybody look now!" and draws my teacher so perilously near the girl with the fearsome boobs he's terrified he'll lose control and drown the poor child in a language of need she can't possibly be expected to understand but nonetheless will find very entertaining

BENEATH THE SUN

They always arrive *in medias res,* logging on to their private epic after writhing down the slippery path into the light of another greeting-card family. "Best wishes!" says mommy-who-holds-it-all-together, gritting her teeth. "We have only one rule here" says the dad, "don't breathe on us after you eat." Intros over, it's time for the game: destined to run the slowest Marathon in history, sonny gives a booing crowd the finger and mouths a fat "fuck you" while his sweetie, dressed in the glittery tan bra and panty set he got her to seal their deal, wins first prize in the Comeliest Chick contest. "Better act now," she whispers, holding her trophies up. "I haven't got forever." And she's right: in a flash the kids are grown and gone and he wonders how long she's been wearing knee-high support hose. Without good looks or races left to run, they sit waiting in front of the TV for their upcoming downfall. After which, an email will be sent to an air-conditioned enclave in the Utah Rockies to be dutifully filed under the heading "Every Person Matters"

FINAL SOLUTION

It's Paradise, alright. But why do the twin hag ticket-takers deny there ever was an amusement park here when I know different. It's freshly-paved, steam is rising from the hot asphalt, we're in my '49 Studebaker with the suicide doors, me and Max Jacob, still wearing his yellow star. "You don't have to keep it on *here*," I tell him, but he only smiles as if he's patting a kid on the head and points to the gold-leaf sign, the kind you see in quaint Vermont towns, only this one reads *Arbeit macht frei*. Holy shit! Did we make a wrong turn? We pass the mansion of the petrochemical magnate rumored to be the brains behind the operation. "He does it with tits and ass," Max tells me "'til you don't know whether to shit or go blind." We've got a lease that guarantees us August-something to death on July-something some year though the fine print is so full of qualifications and disclaimers that Max—who had a year of law school before he found Jesus—tells me effectively negate any rights we might have. "Then what fucking good is it, I want to know?" "Billy, it was just a metaphor to hold back the night," Max says with that indulgent smile—"and a cure for the illusion that you were ever alive." Sure enough, all I see beside me is a rotting pumpkin. Even the armband's gone, along with the lease. Then darkness falls. "Like a curtain," I almost said

FUSION

It happened just like this: I came up behind her in the kitchen and when I reached under her arms to squeeze her nipples the way I always do she giggled and squirmed and pushed me away—me! Playful but determined, I bent to burrow in her thick auburn hair when she turned suddenly as the soup was ready to boil over and in the heat of the moment (not to mention that of the soup) in the cloud of steam and the squirming, the frame of my glasses got hooked on hers which, both of which, in defiance of natural law, began to soften then melt and—lo!—we were joined at the plastic! Her fury knew no limits and with one rage-powered swing she dumped the boiling soup onto my naked genitals (I'd figured why NOT be ready just in case though I should've known better after all the rejections). Needless to say though I'll say it anyway, I screamed so loud the sound carried all the way to my Heavenly Father (a pagan deity and distant relative of Zeus) who at that moment (having often heard my pitiful cries) looked down and, seeing my genitals, like our glasses melting and melding, focused all his powers into one giant whooooosh! and out the window we flashed at electric speed straight to the empyrean where, magically healed, I opened my mouth to thank my H.F. but with upraised hand he stopped me and spoke sternly thus: "Enough of your stupid useless mutual suffering: for the sake of all so-called lovers you shall be memorialized as eternal symbols of the everlasting feud, that often-denied but omnipresent battle of the sexes." And, so saying, snapped his fingers, out of which flew a bolt of lightning that shot our molten, quickly re-configuring "selves" deep into dark space where, still bound to each other at the juncture of our mutual plastics, we became that unique constellation visible in the southern sky at dusk where, fused as we are and bent towards each other, one might think we were locked in an amorous embrace

PARADISE WON

We've gathered to celebrate the end of the project. My huge uptown flat with great views of the bay is jammed with partyers. The food's fine, liquor flows, no one's ugly and the latest Basie band is blowing the world's greatest jazz. When they break, three women, damp with dancing, come towards me smiling. One, a tall blonde in a tiny black dress, presses her breasts against my arm; the second, a full-lipped brunette, caresses her belly in slow circles, looking me right in the eye; while the third, dark and Latin, pulls her thong aside to show her dense pubic hair. The band returns and, on cue, the first trumpet stands and blows a fanfare that transports me, womanless, boozeless, apartmentless, to a mountain peak where I'm sitting like a god in *The Iliad*. Clouds break and the sun appears. Encircled by the mountain's arms, I want nothing

Also Available from saturnalia books:

Arco Iris by Sarah Vap

The Girls of Peculiar by Catherine Pierce

Xing by Debora Kuan

Other Romes by Derek Mong

Faulkner's Rosary by Sarah Vap

Gurlesque: the new grrly, grotesque, burlesque poetics edited by Lara Glenum and Arielle Greenberg

Tsim Tsum by Sabrina Orah Mark

Hush Sessions by Kristi Maxwell

Days of Unwilling by Cal Bedient

Letters to Poets: Conversations about Poetics, Politics, and Community edited by Jennifer Firestone and Dana Teen Lomax

Artist/Poet Collaboration Series:

Velleity's Shade by Star Black / Artwork by Bill Knott
Polytheogamy by Timothy Liu / Artwork by Greg Drasler
Midnights by Jane Miller / Artwork by Beverly Pepper
Stigmata Errata Etcetera by Bill Knott / Artwork by Star Black
Ing Grish by John Yau / Artwork by Thomas Nozkowski
Blackboards by Tomaz Salamun / Artwork by Metka Krasovec

Winners of the Saturnalia Books Poetry Prize:

My Scarlet Ways by Tanya Larkin
The Little Office of the Immaculate Conception by Martha Silano
Personification by Margaret Ronda
To the Bone by Sebastian Agudelo
Famous Last Words by Catherine Pierce
Dummy Fire by Sarah Vap
Correspondence by Kathleen Graber
The Babies by Sabrina Orah Mark

Nowhere Fast was printed using the fonts Benguiatl and Cambria.

www.saturnaliabooks.org